WOMEN SPORTS STARS

Simone Biles
Gymnastics Star

by Lori Mortensen

CAPSTONE PRESS
a capstone imprint

Snap Books are published by Capstone Press,
1710 Roe Crest Drive, North Mankato, Minnesota 56003
www.mycapstone.com

**Cataloging-in-Publication Data is available from the Library of Congress
website.**
ISBN: 978-1-5157-9708-1 (library binding)
ISBN: 978-1-5157-9712-8 (paperback)
ISBN: 978-1-5157-9716-6 (eBook PDF)

Editorial Credits
Abby Colich, editor; Kayla Rossow, designer; Eric Gohl, media researcher;
Katy LaVigne, production specialist

Photo Credits
AP Photo: Houston Chronicle/Smiley N. Pool, 16; Capstone Studio: Karon
Dubke, cover (background); Getty Images: Ronald Martinez, 6–7, Tim Clayton,
23; Newscom: Kyodo, cover, Reuters/Damir Sagolj, 4, 25, Reuters/Mike Blake, 9,
SIPA/Chine Nouvelle, 13, UPI/Kevin Dietsch, 15, ZUMA Press/David Drufke,
21, ZUMA Press/Richard Ulreich, 19; Shutterstock: DFree, 29, Eladora, 8,
hunkmax, 12, Leonard Zhukovsky, 11, 17, 26, 28, Petr Toman, 3

Design Elements: Shutterstock

Printed and bound in the USA.
010780S18

Table of Contents

CHAPTER 1

Moment of Truth

It was August 18, 2011. Fourteen-year-old Simone Biles was competing in the Visa National Championships. A spot on the USA Gymnastics women's artistic Junior National Team was at stake. Out of 50 competitors, only the top 13 would make it. It was the chance of a lifetime.

Simone's heart pounded. She stared up at the huge screen above the arena. After training eight years at Bannon's Gymnastix in Houston, Texas, it came down to this.

As the seconds ticked by, Simone wondered if she was good enough. Earlier, Coach Marta Karolyi told her to perform one of the hardest vaults in the world — the Amanar.

The Amanar launched with a backward handspring. It ended with two-and-a-half twists. Performing a more difficult vault could earn a higher score. But Simone decided she wasn't ready. So she performed the easier Yurchenko. It was the same as the Amanar, except it ended with somersaults instead of twists.

One by one, names flashed on the screen. Simone's name finally appeared. She was stunned. Fourteenth place. She missed making the team by one spot. *One spot.* It was a heartbreaking blow.

GYMNASTICS COMPETITIONS

Each year gymnasts compete at the USA Gymnastics National Championships. Only the top, or elite, gymnasts can compete. Winners from this competition join the National Team. Team members then have the opportunity to compete at the World Championships and the Olympics. The name of the competition changes depending on who the sponsor is.

Almost There

Simone returned to the hotel with her family. Then she broke down and cried. Now she knew — she *wasn't* good enough. She'd let everyone down, including herself. Her family tried to make her feel better, but she only sank deeper into despair.

That night, as she sobbed in the bathroom, her brother called from Texas. What he said helped Simone see things differently. Fourteenth place wasn't the end of the world. It meant she was *almost there*. She was *that good*, and her day would come. This was her year to get better. His words gave Simone hope.

A scene from the 2011 Visa Championship in St. Paul, Minnesota

Since then, Simone has rocked the gymnastics world. She's won four Olympic gold medals. She is also the first female gymnast to win three World Championships — in a row! Competitors agree she's in a league by herself. After racking up 19 international medals, she is the most decorated female gymnast in history.

> ...I missed making the National Team, and I was very sad. I cried a lot. ... So it was very hard, but then it was for the better because I went back to the gym and changed my mind-set.
>
> —Simone Biles interview with Tavis Smiley, December 8, 2016

CHAPTER 2

Backflips and Foster Care

Simone's road to gymnastic superstardom got off to a rocky start. She was born on March 14, 1997, in Columbus, Ohio. Her mother was addicted to drugs and alcohol. Simone was the third of four children. When Simone was 3 years old, social services placed the children in foster care.

Even at age 3, Simone was strong, fast, and fearless. Whatever her older brother did, she did it too. Swing way up high? No problem. Backflips off mailboxes? Easy! As Simone sailed through the air, she felt like she was flying.

A few months after Simone went to foster care, her grandparents took her home to Texas. Ron and Nellie Biles officially adopted Simone when she was 6 years old, along with her little sister. An aunt in Ohio adopted Simone's older siblings.

Ron and Nellie Biles clap as Simone wins an Olympic gold medal in 2016.

FACT

Some gymnasts count as they tumble, twist, and flip through the air to keep track of where they are. Not Simone. She never gets lost.

Field Trip

That summer, Simone went on a field trip that changed her life. Teachers at her day care planned to take the children to visit a farm, but it rained that day. Instead they went to Bannon's Gymnastix down the street. For Simone, it was a dream come true. Suddenly, she was in a gymnasium filled with bars, beams, and vaults. Simone copied the gymnasts' jumping, flipping, and somersaulting, just like she'd copied her brother.

A coach noticed her right away. Who was this small, brave girl tumbling through the air? The coach sent her home with a letter inviting her to take classes. Simone began training on balance beam, uneven bars, floor exercise, and vault twice a week. Soon she was spending three or four hours a day in the gym. Nothing was as thrilling as soaring high in the air and returning to the earth just right.

FACT

Simone began training with Coach Aimee Boorman at Gymnastix when she was 8 years old. To reach elite level, Simone also trained with Marta Karolyi at the same time.

Simone with
Aimee Boorman, 2016

Olympic Dreams

As Simone's skills grew, so did her dreams. When she was 11 years old, she imagined being on the National Team and competing in the Olympics. The 2012 London games were still four years away. And she would only be 15. She had to be 16 to compete. That meant she'd have to wait for the 2016 Olympics, eight years away. By then she'd be 19. Simone knew some gymnasts got injured. They had to quit. Sometimes gymnasts lost their passion for the sport. Would that happen to her?

Simone thought about her future. One night she opened her diary. "I don't know if I will make it," she wrote with a sigh. She turned off the light and tried to sleep. But she couldn't. She opened her diary again. *"I WANT TO GO THE FARTHEST I CAN,"* she added.

FACT

Simone can climb 20 feet (6.1 meters) up a rope in five seconds, using just her arms. It's part of her warm-up.

The 2008 U.S. gymnastics women's team won gold. Watching them inspired Simone.

CHAPTER 3

Perfection

To go the farthest, Simone had to learn more difficult skills. Over the next few years, Simone's efforts paid off. In 2011 Coach Marta Karolyi invited Simone to her gymnastics summer camp. It was a huge step toward Simone's Olympic goals. Karolyi's name was legendary. Her gymnast, Nadia Comaneci, scored the first perfect 10 at the 1976 Montreal Olympics. Another Karolyi gymnast, Mary Lou Retton, did it again at the 1984 Olympics in Los Angeles.

Karolyi's summer camp would be challenging for Simone. Serious gymnasts didn't joke around. They got down to business. Drills, drills, and more drills. "We strive for perfection here," said Karolyi. "If that's not your goal, then you're in the wrong place."

THE KAROLYI COACHES

Marta Karolyi and her husband, Béla, began coaching gymnastics in Romania. The couple moved to the United States in 1981. They became the most successful coaches in American history. They have trained six U.S. national champions, 12 European champions, 15 world champions, and 28 Olympians. Nine of the Olympians won gold.

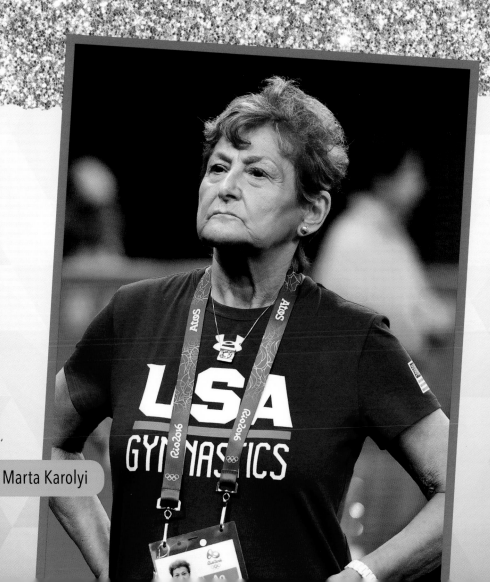

Marta Karolyi

The Karolyi camp, 2011

Tough Choices

Simone knew she was in the right place. She was preparing for the Visa National Championships. She wanted to be on the National Team. The Karolyi camp was her first real taste of what it would take to be a winner. Would all this hard work at Karolyi's camp pay off? A month later at the Visa National Championships, Simone stared at the Jumbotron and got the gut-wrenching news. She did not make the National Team.

The crushing defeat at the National Championships brought Simone to an important fork in the road. She had a big decision to make — step back, or push harder? She was already training 25 to 30 hours a week. To win, she needed more.

At the same time, Simone always wanted to go to high school with her friends. It came down to these two choices. Would she go to high school or work toward the Olympics and be homeschooled? She couldn't do both.

After a lot of tears, Simone made her decision. She'd actually made it long ago. She was ready to give gymnastics everything she had.

"Little Things"

After the 2011 Nationals, Simone returned to the Karolyi camp. Now she was ready. She trained from morning to night, with a three-hour break in between. Perfection meant building up strength and increasing stamina. It meant breaking skills down and perfecting each part. It meant connecting skills so they blended together without a hiccup. It meant mastering the hardest skills in the world, including the Amanar.

"She started to understand that gymnastics is not only about throwing big tricks," said Karolyi. "It's about having patience and working on little things."

Instead of shying away from difficult skills, Simone mastered them. At the 2012 Nationals, she took first place in vault and third in all-around. As she stared at the Jumbotron this time, her face ached from smiling. She came in third overall. She had made the Junior National Team.

COMPETITION SCORING

In 2006 the scoring system for gymnastics competitions changed. It now included a score based on difficulty. Before this change, each gymnast started with 10 points. Judges subtracted points for each error. Now there are two scores. One score for performance is worth up to 10 points. The other score is for difficulty. The harder the skill, the higher start value it has. There is no upper limit. Then scores are added together. Winners usually score 15 points or more.

Simone joins the other top finishers on the podium at the 2012 Visa Nationals.

CHAPTER 4
Mind Games

Simone had made great strides, but there were more challenges ahead. Even with all her wins, Simone struggled with doubts and anxiety. When she was younger, she looked up to her gymnastic idols. Now she was competing against them. She couldn't believe she'd ever be as good as them. Yet when she did win, it only created higher expectations and more pressure. Simone reacted by cutting back on her training.

The result was a disaster. Instead of flying through her routines at the 2013 U.S. Secret Classic in Chicago, Simone was exhausted. She fell off the high bar. She wobbled on the balance beam. She crashed to her knees on her floor routine. Her coach pulled her from the competition. They had a long talk. In spite of the ordeal, her coaches knew Simone could be the best. Karolyi said Simone just needed to "get that head screwed on right."

...it's the beauty of the sport. You have your ups and your downs, and it probably won't be the last time you're going to fall, so you have to get up and try it again.

—Simone Biles interview with *Sunday Edition* on NPR, November 20, 2016

Simone performs her beam routine during the U.S. Secret Classic on July 27, 2013.

Go Have Fun

Simone began meeting with sports psychologist Robert Andrews. With his help, she learned how to relax and forget about other people's expectations. He helped her remember why she was there in the first place. She loved gymnastics because it was *fun*.

Three weeks later, Simone competed at the 2013 P&G National Championships. It was a complete turnaround. Now that she had found the fun again, everything fell into place. Simone exploded through her daring routines. She racked up medals in all four individual events.

THE BILES

During the floor routine at the 2013 Nationals, Simone astonished the arena. She showed off a new tumbling pass – a double layout with a half-twist. She'd made it up by accident one day as she gave her strained calf muscle a break on a blind, backward landing. Since she was the first one to do it at a World Championship, the trick was named after her – the Biles.

FACT

Out of all of Simone's events – floor, balance beam, vault, and uneven bars – floor is her favorite. Because she is short and has small hands, her weakest event is uneven bars.

Simone was all smiles at the 2013 P&G National Championships.

CHAPTER 5

Making History

After Simone's success at the 2013 Nationals, she was unstoppable. The next year, she won the U.S. and world titles in the all-around competition. When she returned to the U.S. Secret Classic, she swept the gold in vault, floor exercise, balance beam, and the all-around. In 2015 her awards continued to pile up. At the World Championships in Glasgow, Scotland, she won a team gold, golds in floor and balance beam, and a bronze on the vault. Simone was the first female to win three world all-around titles three years in a row.

FACT

Simone is scared of bees. The whole world found out at the 2014 World Championships. She was standing on the podium when another winner pointed out a bee in her bouquet. Simone dropped her flowers and scrambled to get away.

Now the 2016 Olympics were in Simone's reach. To make the team, she had to compete at the Olympic trials. Simone took first place. That night Coach Karolyi named Simone to the Olympic team along with four others. They nicknamed themselves "The Final Five." It was a tribute to Coach Karolyi. The legendary coach planned to retire at the end of the season. Without her daily guidance, none of them would be there. The rules would be changing too. Instead of five gymnasts, future Olympics would only allow four members per team.

Marta Karolyi addresses "The Final Five" prior to the 2016 Olympics in Rio de Janeiro, Brazil.

A Dream Come True

Eight years had passed since Simone wrote about her Olympic dreams in her diary. Now she was stepping into the Olympic arena. The entire world would be watching. Simone's heart pounded with excitement. To calm her jitters, she told herself, *Just like practice*.

Simone was ready. Her level of difficulty was high. So high that it put her start scores ahead of the competition before she even began. Flashing a smile, Simone flew higher, spun faster, and moved through her routines effortlessly. She rarely made a mistake. A lower start score on her uneven bar routine let a Russian gymnast pull ahead briefly. Soon, however, Simone was back in the lead. At one point during the beam finals, Simone had to steady herself. But the mistake didn't matter. Simone was in a category by herself. She won Olympic gold medals for team, all-around, vault, and floor. She won bronze on beam.

> We're out there for less than 10 minutes, and you prepare your whole life for this. I knew the expectations were there, but I can only control what I do, not what anyone else wants me to do.
> —Simone Biles interview with *Glamour* as one of their Women of the Year, 2016

FACT

At 4 feet, 8 inches (142.24 centimeters) tall, Simone was the shortest of all 555 U.S. Olympic athletes in Rio.

New Dreams

Simone went the farthest she could. She has rocked the gymnastic world. After earning a staggering five Olympic and 14 World Championship medals, Simone is the most winning American gymnast in history. Some say she is the best gymnast of all time.

Simone has checked the 2016 Olympics off her wish list. Now she is taking time off and exploring new dreams. "She's been totally dedicated," said Coach Boorman. "I just want her to love life."

FACT

When Simone is not training, she likes to play with her four German shepherds – Maggie, Atlas, Lily, and Bella. She also enjoys Sunday dinners with her family and watching Netflix.

Simone is off to a great start. She recently wrote a book about her life, *Courage to Soar: A Body in Motion, A Life in Balance* with *The New York Times* bestselling author Michelle Burford. She's also put her dancing skills to the test on TV's *Dancing with the Stars*. Simone returned to the gym in August 2017 to begin training for the 2020 Olympics in Tokyo. When she arrives, she'll be ready to win. She'll have plenty of fun along the way too.

Simone at the *Glamour* Women of the Year Awards on November 14, 2016

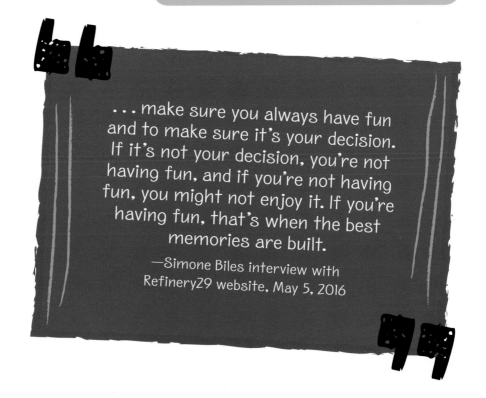

. . . make sure you always have fun and to make sure it's your decision. If it's not your decision, you're not having fun, and if you're not having fun, you might not enjoy it. If you're having fun, that's when the best memories are built.

—Simone Biles interview with Refinery29 website, May 5, 2016

Timeline

1997 ·· born in Columbus, Ohio

2000 ·· Simone and siblings put in foster care

2003 ·· Simone and her sister officially adopted by
her grandparents, Ron and Nellie Biles

·· goes on a field trip to Bannon's Gymnastix
in Houston, Texas

2005 ·· begins training with Aimee Boorman

2006 ·· gymnastic scoring system changes, rewarding
difficult skills

2008 ·· dreams of Olympics and writes her goal in
her diary

2011 ·· invited to Karolyi's gymnastic summer camp

·· fails to make Junior National team at
the Visa National Championships in St. Paul,
Minnesota

·· chooses between high school and homeschooling

2012 ·· earns spot on the Junior National Team

2013 ·· pulled from 2013 U.S. Secret Classic competition

·· meets with sports psychologist

·· begins winning streak at 2013 P&G National
Championships

2016 ·· wins four medals at 2016 Olympics at
Rio de Janeiro

2017 ·· returns to the gym in August after taking
time off

Read More

Fishman, Jon M. *Simone Biles*. Sports All-Stars. Minneapolis: Lerner, 2017.

Hansen, Grace. *Simone Biles*. Olympic Biographies. Minneapolis: Abdo Kids, 2017.

McAneney, Caitie. *Simone Biles: Greatest Gymnast of All Time*. Breakout Biographies. New York: PowerKids, 2018.

Internet Sites

Use FactHound to find Internet sites related to this book.

Visit *www.facthound.com*

Just type in 9781515797081 and go!

 Check out projects, games and lots more at **www.capstonekids.com**

Index